faim

© 2016 by Samuel Vaden

Printed in the United States of America

All rights reserved. No part of the book may be used or reproduced in the any manner whatsoever without written permission from the author except in the case of brief quotations embodied in presentations, articles and reviews.

Library of Congress Cataloging-in-Publication Data in on file at the Library of Congress, Washington, DC.

ISBN-13: 978-0692708026 (Art of Living Publications)
ISBN-10: 0692708022

www.samuelvaden.com

To my mother, father and sister, who never abandoned me in my times of need. You taught me the true meaning of family, unconditional love and perspective. Everything I do is for you.

Thank you for allowing me to "fly" and embark on my adventure to California for the past 3 years. I needed the space and personal time to reflect on what had transpired over the course of thirteen years. I was able to reconcile a tremendous amount of internal turmoil, pain, regret and shame.

Now I have nothing left to hide, nothing to lose and I have reached clarity. The freedom I am experiencing is a breath of fresh air. Don't worry, your son and brother will be coming home a lot sooner than you think.

--

In memory of Pépère and Elissa. Qu'ils reposent en paix. Thank you for watching over me in my times of need. I hope that I have made you proud. One day we will all be celebrating together with larger than life smiles in the sky above.

--

To the silent warriors, male and female, in our uniformed services and those that who are no longer serving. True strength is speaking up and seeking help. After reading this book, you will understand what I mean.

It is possible to overcome what seems impossible.

faim

Samuel Vaden

"I decided it is better to scream. Silence is the real crime against humanity."

— Nadezhda Mandelstam

Introduction

faim.

One word with so many personal meanings. One word that has defined my existence for 13 years. One word that has directly impacted my life and has affected every personal relationship I have stepped into and then exited. One word that has influenced every career change I have pursued, every adventure I have gone on and every path I have walked. It has taken 13 years for the meaning of this one word to evolve from being the darkest moment in my life to being the most freeing.

I am an Anorexia Nervosa and Body Dysmorphic Disorder survivor. I am lucky to be alive and I have never been more thankful.

Thirteen years ago in 2003, I was a young 18 year-old plebe entering the United States Military Academy at West Point. I had spent the previous 12 years dreaming of following in my father's footsteps to join the Long Grey Line and cement my place in its illustrious history. I vividly remember flipping through my father's West Point yearbook at an early age; so much so, that the pages were falling out. I knew by heart the exact pages where my father's face would show up. I couldn't wait to rush to those pages and stare in awe.

My father had to pry me from the living room carpet to bring me to bed and I would beg him to tell me stories about his experiences. Every time I opened that book, I felt closer to him. I never felt more connected to the man who I admired than when my face was deep into the weathered pages of grim-faced men and military history.

It took 12 years of dreaming, persistence and hard work to open my acceptance letter in front of my proud parents. It took less than 1 year as a cadet at West Point to lose it all. It took less than 1 year for a 210-lb, 18 year-old male who came from an amazing, loving family to shrivel into a 134-lb malnourished skeleton of his former self who struggled with self-worth, self-identity and a distorted image of the male human body.

I still remember the rainy, cold morning on February 7th, 2004 as if it were yesterday. It was the day I was officially discharged from the US Army. I was standing on the curb next to Grant Hall on the campus of West Point, shivering in civilian clothes waiting for my taxi to bring me to the airport. I was shivering from the below-freezing temperatures and malnutrition. However, I knew deep down inside that the intensity of the shaking also stemmed from the shame, anxiety and paranoia of the inevitable barrage of inquiries that were coming my way.

As I stood on the icy sidewalk, all I could see were the faces of the men from my father's yearbook diverting their gazes from my unsteady, tear-filled eyes. All I could see were the eyes of my father seared into my mind, judging me. As the rain hit my shoulders and my body tensed from the wind off of the Hudson River, I felt a rush of emotions that I couldn't understand. All I could do was stand there. Bare. Vulnerable. Hungry.

In the blink of an eye, I had let my dream slip from my grasp and was left helpless to decipher emotions I couldn't understand. I had no one to talk to, I was embarrassed and ashamed. I couldn't talk to the Army, I couldn't talk to my parents and I couldn't talk to my friends. I internalized everything, I blamed myself for not living up to everyone's expectations and for failing them.

In my attempt to become the ultimate soldier in the eyes of the US Army and to become a "real man" in the eyes of society, I danced with death. I had no idea what I was doing at the time. I had created a new normal for myself and it was literally starting to kill me.

I had rationalized in my young mind that by adhering to a very strict diet of canned tuna, water and black coffee, I would transform my body into the poster child of the Army. In my mind, I was obsessed with achieving a sub-4% body fat percentage, working out 3-4 times a day at the expense of my studies and adhering to an absolute zero-carb/high-protein eating plan. I genuinely believed that my "proactive" regimen would place me in the top 1% of all the cadets taking the Army Physical Fitness Test and that I would become more masculine in the eyes of my peers.

I was obsessed with excessive, purposeless, physical activity that ended up being a detriment, rather than a benefit, to my health and well-being. I would look in the mirror every time I passed a bathroom or I would sneak a discrete glance towards the classroom windows lining the hallways to ascertain if I had achieved the physique I had materialized in my head. I had trained myself to spot a "flaw" (that didn't really exist) and do everything in my power to try to "fix it". Instead of focusing on the positive aspects of my body and my personality, I spent countless hours obsessing over an illusionary physique complex.

I created more anxiety from my body disorder/anorexia nervosa than I did from the typical West Point cadet hazing. The irony. I wasn't fazed by the upperclassmen, the non-commissioned officers yelling in my face or the infamous Chemistry Lab that dropped everyone's 1st semester GPA. Instead, I was more terrified of imperfections of the human body that might possibly make me less competitive in the eyes of the US Army.

Consequently, my compulsive athletic activity, body dysmorphic disorder and anorexia nervosa altered my body's physiology. In a matter of 6 months, I had triggered an immunosuppression "acute phase" response, a decreased anabolic testosterone response, an increased catabolic response, an increased central serotonin response, a loss of emotional vigor, an inhibited lactic acid response, a decreased maximum oxygen uptake, hypothalamic dysfunction and adrenal exhaustion.

In simple terms: my immune system was shutting down, my muscles were wasting away and I was losing essential fatty tissues to protect my vital organs. I became less emotional, more apathetic and my lung capacities were drastically diminished. I altered the gland in my brain that controls everything in the body. The hypothalamus' primary function is homeostasis, which is to maintain the body's status quo system-wide. I threw that little guy into a whirlwind and it affected everything.

It's like throwing a delicate piece of clothing into the fastest wash cycle possible: at some point during the cycle, the clothing starts to tear, shred, lose color and no longer looks the same. You know it's the piece of clothing from the beginning of the wash cycle, but it'll never be the same.

Over the course of 13 years, I experienced depression and I cried in secret without anyone to confide in. I eventually found solace in music and reembraced writing to shed the shame, failure and anxiety little by little. It took me hitting rock bottom financially, going through a divorce at the age of 27, and physically relocating 3,000 miles from my loving family and friends in 2013 to reach clarity.

I jumped off the cliff and spread my wings, not knowing if I'd land on solid ground. I plunged off that cliff, hitting a few rocks and bumps on the way down; however, I regained my composure and my wings. While some of the psychological experiences will linger with me forever, I accept that it was a part of evolving as a human being. I am happy with my body today, focusing on being healthy and happy rather than obsessing about a "look". I see everything in a new light and have put everything into perspective.

I learned a level of love for humankind that I never knew existed, the type of passion that never subsides. I discovered a passion that grows exponentially and in different directions. I realized the power we each hold in our behavior, our words, our smiles, our kisses, our hugs and our eyes. I realized that we all have skeletons and personal baggage. The pivotal and freeing moment is when we wear those badges proudly and make them part of our character without fear of judgment.

I am grateful for the experiences that have textured my mind, body and soul. Without these experiences, I would not be where I am today. I am at peace and have absolute clarity as to why I am on this Earth. I am here to help others heal and to be a positive reminder of recovery. *faim* is my promise to the world to be as vulnerable as possible, a poetic representation of 13 years' worth of emotions.

The reader will notice that I have omitted a Table of Contents and that I chose not to provide titles for my poems. I did this on purpose, as I did not want to bias the reader and create a narrow tunnel of interpretation. These poems are based on my personal experiences; however, I wanted to write them so that each and every reader could find themselves in the universality of love, sadness, loyalty, pain, suffering, guilt, joy, confusion and enlightenment.

When I write my poetry, I never edit, manipulate or change the words that fall upon the page. If it came from my mind, it stays there untouched. It would be an injustice to the reader to cover the rawness and vulnerability of my words with a safe veneer.

Possibly one day, I will elaborate on each and every one of these experiences in greater detail in an autobiography or another work of literature. It is my sincere hope to reach children and adults through my public speaking and outreach in the coming weeks and months. If I can touch one person with my story and my words, and help them on their road to recovery and clarity, then it was worth everything.

Part of my commitment to this issue is to raise money in order to help women and men seek the psychological and medical help they so desperately need. In order to make this a reality, I am donating 25% of the net proceeds from the sale of *faim* to Project HEAL.

The mission of Project HEAL is to provide grant funding for people with eating disorders who cannot afford treatment, promote healthy body image and self-esteem, and serve as a testament that full recovery from an eating disorder is possible. For more information on Project HEAL, please visit www.theprojectheal.org.

This issue is near to my heart, please help me in my effort to shed light on this prevalent issue and positively impact the lives of brave women and men around the world battling the psychological and physiological wounds of body dysmorphic disorder, anorexia nervosa and bulimia.

I chose to use poetry as my initial canvas, because it was (and is) my therapy. You are reading the most intimate manifestations of my mind and heart. Poetry was my therapy during my darkest days. Poetry is now my steady hand in an unpredictable world.

faim.

Hunger.

Samuel Vaden

Anorexia Nervosa in Males[1]

Anorexia nervosa is a severe, life-threatening disorder in which the individual refuses to maintain a minimally normal body weight, is intensely afraid of gaining weight, and exhibits a significant distortion in the perception of the shape or size of his body, as well as dissatisfaction with his body shape and size.

Behavioral Characteristics:

Excessive dieting, fasting, restricted diet
Food rituals
Preoccupation with body building, weight lifting, or muscle toning
Compulsive exercise
Difficulty eating with others, lying about eating
Frequently weighing self
Preoccupation with food
Focus on certain body parts; e.g., buttocks, thighs, stomach
Disgust with body size or shape
Distortion of body size; i.e., feels fat even though others tell him he is already very thin

Emotional and Mental Characteristics:

Intense fear of becoming fat or gaining weight
Depression
Social isolation
Strong need to be in control
Rigid, inflexible thinking, "all or nothing"
Decreased interest in sex or fears around sex
Possible conflict over gender identity or sexual orientation
Low sense of self-worth—uses weight as a measure of worth
Difficulty expressing feelings
Perfectionistic -- strives to be the neatest, thinnest, smartest, etc.
Difficulty thinking clearly or concentrating
Irritability, denial -- believes others are overreacting to his low weight or caloric restriction
Insomnia

Physical Characteristics:

Low body weight (15% or more below what is expected for age, height, activity level)

---

[1] "Anorexia Nervosa in Males." N.p., n.d. Web. 2 Apr. 2016.
<http://www.nationaleatingdisorders.org/anorexia-nervosa-males>.

Lack of energy, fatigue
Muscular weakness
Decreased balance, unsteady gait
Lowered body temperature, blood pressure, pulse rate
Tingling in hands and feet
Thinning hair or hair loss
Lanugo (downy growth of body hair)
Heart arrhythmia
Lowered testosterone levels

"6.8% of active duty men struggle with bulimia, 2.5% with anorexia, and 40.8% with unspecified eating disorders. American servicewomen are 6-10 times more likely to develop bulimia than their civilian cohort. Beyond that, 63% of enlisted women suffer from unspecified eating disorders-illnesses that cause significant impairment or distress." [2]

These are the ones who stepped forward. Imagine the staggering number of men and women who are too afraid, ashamed and embarrassed to seek help. I was. Our government and military needs to create a new standard of "true strength" for our service members. The strength to build self-worth, the strength to love oneself unconditionally, the strength to trust in their personal relationships to facilitate constructive communication and the strength to provide the resources to the men and women who need it the most.

Body dysmorphic disorder, anorexia nervosa and bulimia are, first and foremost, psychological disorders. They often lead to dire physiological consequences for the individual. Those suffering and recovering from body dysmorphic disorder, anorexia nervosa and bulimia never wanted to hurt themselves and/or their loved ones. They need help, they need understanding and a safe place to communicate their worries, fears and yearning for healing. My hope is that we can continue to educate the population on these disorders, inspire community involvement and create a respectful platform regardless of gender and age to hash out these issues affecting millions of people each year.

---

[2] "Eating Disorders in the Veteran Population." Center for Discovery Blog. N.p., 16 Nov. 2015. Web. 02 Apr. 2016. <https://www.centerfordiscovery.com/blog/eating-disorders-in-the-veteran-population/>.

THE COLLECTION

Note to the reader: The symbol "_" denotes the end of each poem

these chains know the cold of my unrest
but I know the warmth of my own skin
I know the balance of where the lips part
is held hostage by a self-denying
paranoia
an ego built on false pretenses
and loose sand

the pale existence
of a lingering shadow
still covers a portion of the ground where I look
down, waiting
pacing its movement
on the pulse of my eyes
which close in symmetry

I eagerly await the darkness of my skin
the oblique canvas
that absorbs the light on the outside
of my world
I interpret the light as it glances over my eyelids
studying the patterns
rather than reaching out

I rest in my qualms
and become a student
of the world, blind
I feel more
with less and less

—

if you have it in you
breathe harder
so that I can float
on the anticipation of greedy gallows
and the remnants
of a lost love

let me savor
this moment of adrenaline
and lust

let me watch
this painting run
with its watercolors fleeing
the salty rivers
and the angry crest

do not attempt to save
me, please
on this descent
with my head above water
for I have ignored the pain
of the freezing cold
below the surface

I still have the warmth
of the world through
my eyes
that makes the landing
graceful

—

how such a small object
can control
the screams inside
this large life
in uniform
my uniformity
fell apart
at the seams of my fabric
that held the love
for my father

one over, one under
the details of the weave
clinched together
tighter
to cover the
gaps of weakness
unprepared to own
his audience
and the ones standing watch behind him

—

my nature
is to be steady
this, my loved ones
assume

yet, the palm of this hand
trembles
in privacy
cradling the memory
of every sound

escaping the lips of
the adolescents
walking by me

my next thought
becomes unsteady
as my head snaps
to the distant horizon
the heat of the memory
burns inside of me

and intensifies
the sounds
of the little ones I made promises to

their pleading stares
linger in unison
wanting answers
unaware that my silence
speaks more volume
than the empty words
that would have lapsed
the ridges of my lips
to calm my guilt
and relax the qualms
of my conscious

—

I wonder
whether the torn
cloth
around the window
was from the wind outside
or from my own tempest

I've sat here
silent
for how long, I don't know

the crevices
of my chair
ache from the weight
of the heavy thoughts
that sit full
yet unbalanced
upon my head

I wonder if the mirror
is playing tricks with my mind?
it masterfully
manipulates light
capturing small amounts
and bringing them
halfway
to my presence

my eyes see the
entirety

my eyes have no fingers
I cannot reach
I cannot hold

the rays of light
tease my senses
they resemble

iron bars
the matter, matters not
the strength of its symbolism
prevents my escape

—

is it normal to stand in sand, mouth open
expecting air to fill your lungs
but find yourself choking on freedom?

textured by memories
that washed ashore
frigid thighs, toned

pillared by brute strength burdened by a dense
heavy atmosphere
and evidenced by the trails of lines burrowing down
a forehead
mapping deep worries towards both eyes
which hold so much emotion

finding oneself squinting
with hopes of making the picture clearer
removing the fog from curved windows
and pulling whatever lights remains from the world

inside, locking it away
and falling asleep fast
pinning the chin against the throat
closing its escape

lips pursed
satisfied, and safe, with the thought of owning
something so complex in theory

yet simple in emotion

standing still in time
buying moments
bracing firmly, knowing the cold water
will maneuver around those pillars
and leave the light
in a deserving place

—

there was natural sunlight
two people, sitting across from each other
no words spoken
but
the pressure of their breath
spoke volumes
trepidation
fragility

they were surrounded by supportive silhouettes
tears flowing
their eyes sheltered by the bare branches
of the trees lining the patio

the wind calmed
the intense silence
beckoned the subtle light
to warm his neck
and ease her pain

the minute passed
his throat tightened with each
swallow
the rawness stings

a real feeling
powerful

he opened his eyes
and woke from the dream

he orients himself
steadies his gaze
a tear falls, loudly

he sees a white dove
facing the ocean
with its back to him

a mere foot away
oblivious to the heavy breathing and shuddering
heartbeat
the rush of adrenaline
and the confusion
screaming from inside the hollows of his heart

he felt like the loneliest person in the world
helpless, unable to make sense
of the dove
and the silence lingering in his mind
from the dream

he lies down again
forcing his eyes to close, hard
hoping to fall asleep
and wake up to an empty balcony

his eyes snap open
he doesn't move
or dare tilt his head towards the balcony
he's afraid of the symbol
and what it might represent
intuitively, he knows he is not in control
it frightens him, it drains him

then it happened

his face fell to the left
as if a hand from heaven
gracefully cupped his head
and ushered his cheek towards the window

he remembered staring at the dove
the sheets of his bed
soaked from the tears
that fell uncontrollably from his eyes

a lone white dove
standing guard while he slept
choosing not to abandon him
while he struggled with shallow breaths

he can't cry anymore
his heart has slowed
to a near stand still
he lets out a deep breath
and drifts off
he surrenders
to the world

no coincidences
bared souls
more tears
new smiles

manifestation
of dreams
and forgiveness

we are not in control
he murmured
as the dove flew off

a piece of him left
with the dove
what remained
came to define
a man
stronger

—

seeing
he said
would cure the aches
of anxiety
and lessen the burden
of the foreboding

love's curse

tightening the breadth of his effort
to mask the input
of his circle
reflecting, deflecting
his intuitions
for hopes that they won't
weigh down the cracks
forming on the sides of the his fragile
balance

defending, pretending
that the mornings of staring in the mirror
were nothing more than insecurities
when in fact
the look in his swollen eyes
blurred by tears
saw more truth in their lifetime
than the person
who gave them life

—

what if?
the closer we come
and the further we reach

we create a space
where an embrace
feels the agony
and pulse of love
forbidden

and imprisoned
by time passed
and assumptions made
imagine
what the sheets hold
stories written within our souls

where the heart fights the urge
to ask for credit
of faithfulness
in a time where desires present themselves, abundant
and one stayed true

what if?
my want, my need
was validation for a feeling
feeling for validation

mirror within a mirror
false assumptions
opening
conversation
leading to true confirmations
so is the confirmation the end?
or the beginning of the next reflection?
in which we discover how long we are willing to stare at oneself?
am I waiting for her, or for myself?

—

you grabbed my heart
squeezing with anger, frustration
deep sadness, overwhelming anxiety
tightening your grip
curling your fingers
digging, grasping, clutching

you couldn't look me in my eyes
instead you were concentrating on a focal point
on the wall behind my head
hoping that the room would stop spinning
that the world would make sense again
and one could gingerly step out of the free fall
or burst violently out of the dream
a disguised and disfigured nightmare
rising out of the swell
that had been forming for a long time
birthed as a disruption of the plates
slowly and menacingly evolving into a festering of currents

approaching from a distance
yet we stood fragile and silent
knowing very well that the shell
would not, could not
withstand the impact
almost accepting with apathy
the cracks forming would engulf our bodies

squeeze harder, let me be your release
I will not flinch, nor cry
I will gently lift your chin
brush the tears from your cheek
and look into your eyes
I will take hold of your wrist
pulling it in closer
I will swallow the pressure for both of us

tighten that grip

drain it please
allow me to be your release
I beg of you
let go, set yourself free
so that the swell only takes with it
one soul
the ocean's pariah
love's martyr
even as I get dragged away
I will face you
so you can see
a smile evident in my eyes

I will gently whisper
not an apology
not a song of sorrow
only bits of raw emotion
shaped by the winds
filtered by the sand

if it reaches you
it will be a message of enlightenment and growth
if it returns
at the behest of the wind
I will embrace the will of that which
we cannot control
and I will continue to live and love

—

she calmly walks down the hallway
her olive skin and long legs
gracefully interrupt the silence

held by the stillness of the night

candles greet her presence
and the reflection of fire
greets their phoenix
waiting for her return

the rope
stands tall
willing to burn itself

to bestow humility
showing its dying love
in its purest form
to the one
who lit the inferno

if she speaks
the heat
intensifies
breathing, gasps

the science
of air
deepens the effect
of love
and imminent death

we heal
harden our seal
resurrect
for love's mark
again and again

—

if by chance the restlessness
of my fingers
awoke the clarity of your desires
then open your eyes
like your heart moments ago.

let your wildest imaginations
be unfettered and pure

see through the things
that catch your eye
and live in the moments
that linger in the fading light

—

do you see me
here in the shade?

with my elbow resting
on the arm
of this salvaged
wood
surely weathered
by its own torrents
and rough seasons

do you see the
concentration
and passion in my eyes?
with the three fingers
closest to heaven
propping up my chin
in alignment
so as not to lose my view
the posture
of an animal
in deep thought
and simultaneous
hunt

do you see
my heel
fighting gravity?
the excitement
in its tension
and inability
to hide
its intentions

the room
has a bourbon
glow
its warm rings

embrace the walls
fingers that tap
the tables
and seek adventure
below them
—

this is where he is now, laying bare at your feet
his soul, stretched wide
fastened onto the wind, taking with it
any restlessness and quivering lips
finding solace at the place where emotions
embrace their vulnerability
and the character of their truest form
endears them to everyone
for he has turned himself inside out
allowing people to walk over his canvas

he bides his time
and teaches himself in silence
of the context which precedes the storm
and of what follows the release of any inhibitions
he lets the wind pick him up again
this time flirting with the jagged edges of a precipice
accepting that he may be torn
and that he will leave a part of himself
to be held captive by the high altitude and violent teeth of the bluff
when will the wind pick him up again?

he will look back, over his shoulder
when the time comes
he will focus on that piece of himself
and then turn his head into the wind
allowing the vast unknown in front of him
to define what remains of his body, his heart, his soul

—

heavy expectations, he stops mid stride
uneased by the ease
with which people give advice
leverage to build self-righteousness
ignorant to their own hidden passions
the louder they scream and the more often, the narcotic effect
becomes their reality

their power rests in proclamations, their weakness in false confidence
their hunger never satisfied, their promises are ropes
long enough to let you walk into your own restraint
your inhibitions bolster their relaxed grip, momentarily
for they have become experts, quickly
mastering the manipulations, which glean the most gain
dismissing the known losses, diminishing the value of their child-like innocence

their genuine humanity, forgotten
all the while audiences become mesmerized, a sea of blank faces
unable to make creases around their lips, never experiencing

a real smile
a true fulfillment
a passionate release, greater than ever experienced

they are more concerned with landing on both feet firmly
rather than naturally, gracefully
connecting with the ground and letting oneself go
we ask for the audience's forgiveness
for possibly stimulating thoughts, questioning the orthodox
possibly endangering the little freedom they have

but what is a little release now,
when being true to yourself
provides the truest escape
the purest embrace
with the longest lasting freedom

we warn the puppet masters, the quick prophets
that the chains, which torment the hearts and minds yearning for more
will break eventually

and through tears, sweat and heartache
they will showcase the best that freedom offers

they will turn around, standing boldly
and you will see, in great detail
the smile, and the creases on their face

—

no human life
in its breaths, in its heaves
can be measured by a singular point in time
for it is constrained by parameters
and thrown viciously
by unbalanced emotions

jubilance

razed by sorrow
held up by
the audiences' projections of burrowed hope
mere facades of a soul moving forward
constructed of fragile smiles
where any change in the speed
of their support

tear down souls and tethered hopes
leaving the individual holding onto a single rope with a fierce grip
from a bridge, one existing without land on each side
just there, a superficial monolith, solemnly supporting the weight of a person
with the world on his shoulders, trying to focus on one thing
survival

—

detached from reality, a man sits
high and vast above the clouds
looking down, chin resting where his heart beats
one hand calm and still, the other trembles in angst
he reaches through the cool air, the change in temperature
stings his skin, gravitating towards the warmth of the ground
far below, beyond his vision

earnestly grasping at the wind
the rain
the ocean

he accepts that whatever he touches, he was meant to touch
and accepts that his hand might be lost
but he knows with certainty
that he will continue to reach, to feel
for the search and adventure is what keeps his heart beating

and his one hand still

—

in my details
the shallow
waters perspire

the day after next
evaporates
quickly
the moisture
clings to my elbows
and the edge
of my fingertips

gracefully
clenching my teeth
and biting my lips
kissing death
to digest my convictions
and to placate my stress

in distress
I challenge my class
with which I learn
and teach the world

the inside of my mouth
tastes like chalk
and the outline
of my body
becomes the lesson

—

a frailty
misunderstood
beckoned
his hubris
pulling from the shadows
just that

a weightless matter
that mattered
to him

unbeknown to his senses
the ode to his tragedy
was sung
with notes
that tightened

his hauteur
draped over his shoulders
by robed minds
and pressed hearts

#

Samuel Vaden has spent the past 15 years working in various music entertainment, real estate and technology-related endeavors. He is the co-founder of two early-stage/stealth-mode startup ventures in California and Florida, respectively. Samuel is also a commercial real estate advisor in California and Florida. He utilizes personal earnings from his commercial real estate endeavors to fund his entrepreneurial efforts and to support worthwhile causes which advocate for U.S. military veterans' issues, the prevention of cyber-bullying and those organizations that raise awareness for individuals affected by body image/eating disorders.

Diversification of revenue streams and charitable efforts has always been part of Samuel's *modus operandi*. Samuel strongly embraces the concept of "Never Put All Your Eggs in One Basket," wholeheartedly championing the notion that one should plant numerous "intellectual property seeds" across several professional industries and areas of personal interest with the goal of nurturing them to grow into positive and profitable ventures.

He earned his Master's in Business Administration from American University in Washington, D.C with concentrations in Integrated Marketing Communications and Real Estate Finance. He spent his undergraduate years at the United States Military Academy in West Point, NY and Roanoke College in Salem, VA where he graduated with a Bachelor's in Business Administration in 2007. He currently splits his time between California and Florida.

For more information, please visit www.samuelvaden.com and follow Samuel on his Twitter/IG social media feeds at the handle @SirVaden.

www.ingramcontent.com/pod-product-compliance
Lightning Source LLC
Chambersburg PA
CBHW061346040426
42444CB00011B/3116